Old Economy Village

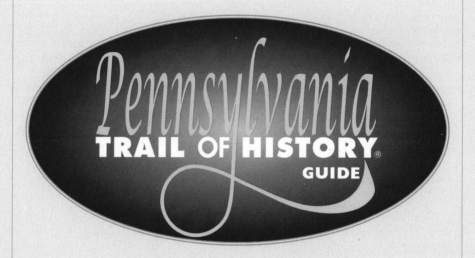

Text by Daniel B Reibel
Photographs by Art Becker

STACKPOLE BOOKS

PENNSYLVANIA HISTORICAL
AND MUSEUM COMMISSION

Kyle R. Weaver, Series Editor
Tracy Patterson, Designer

Published by
STACKPOLE BOOKS
5067 Ritter Road
Mechanicsburg, Pennsylvania 17055

Printed in the United States of America
2 4 6 8 10 9 7 5 3 1
FIRST EDITION

Maps by Caroline Stover

Photography
Art Becker: 3, 5, 12, 26, 27, 30–47
Commonwealth Media Services: cover

Library of Congress Cataloging-in-Publication Data

Reibel, Daniel B.
  Old Economy Village : Pennsylvania trail of history guide / text by Daniel B Reibel.— 1st ed.
    p. ; cm.—(Pennsylvania trail of history guides)
  Includes bibliographical references.
  ISBN 0-8117-2957-5
  1. Harmony Society—History. 2. Old Economy Village (Ambridge, Pa.)—History. 3. Old Economy Village (Ambridge, Pa.)—Guidebooks. I. Pennsylvania Historical and Museum Commission. II. Title. III. Series.

HX656.H2 R45 2002
974.8'92—dc21   2002019743

Contents

Editor's Preface

William Penn's experiment of religious toleration made Pennsylvania, in the eighteenth century, a haven for a diversity of persecuted groups from Europe. Such immigrants continued to trickle into Pennsylvania after ratification of the Constitution and its subsequent First Amendment, which guaranteed religious freedom to all people in the new republic. Among the later immigrants were the Harmonists, who established a communal society in western Pennsylvania in the nineteenth century and enjoyed not only the right to worship as they pleased but also substantial industrial success. The Pennsylvania Historical and Museum Commission (PHMC) preserves the remains of the Harmonist culture at Old Economy Village—and in this new volume of the Pennsylvania Trail of History Guides, Stackpole Books is pleased to join the PHMC to tell the story of this remarkable group that became a leader in the Industrial Revolution in Pennsylvania.

This series of handbooks on the historic sites and museums administered by the PHMC was conceived and created by Stackpole Books with the cooperation of the PHMC's Division of Publications and Bureau of Historic Sites and Museums. Donna Williams heads the latter, and she and her staff of professionals review the text of each guidebook for accuracy and have made many valuable recommendations. Diane Reed, Chief of Publications, has facilitated relations between the PHMC and Stackpole from the project's inception, organized the review process with the commission, and attended to numerous details related to the venture.

For this volume, Mary Ann Landis, Director of Old Economy Village, met with me to develop the outline for the guidebook and ensured that the most recent interpretation of the Harmonist culture was reflected in the text. The staff at Old Economy helped with many of the fine details of the project. Art Becker added his distinctive touch with his photography of the Harmonist structures and artifacts.

Daniel B Reibel, the author of the text, was Director of Old Economy from 1965 to 1981, has been Director of Washington Crossing Historic Park and Director of Landis Valley Museum, and served as the Administrator of the Eastern Region Historic Sites for the PHMC. He has written extensively on the Harmonists and Old Economy Village and continues in that course here with an account of the rise and fall of the Harmony Society and an armchair tour of their third and final home, where they achieved economic success and lived out their version of Utopia.

Kyle R. Weaver, Editor
Stackpole Books

Introduction to the Site

O ld Economy Village, built between 1824 and 1831, housed a religious community known as the Harmony Society. The site in Ambridge, Pennsylvania, preserves the hub of the Society's religious, social, cultural and economic life. The group that became the Society was formed in Germany in 1785 by George Rapp and came to America in 1803. Before founding Economy, the group built two other towns in the United States, both called Harmony, one in Pennsylvania and the other in Indiana Territory. The members shared the belief that the Millennium—the coming of God's thousand-year reign—was imminent and that in preparation for it, they should lead a life similar to what they would lead in heaven. The community practiced a form of Christian communitarianism, sharing all their possessions equally. Their religious beliefs also included adult baptism, celibacy, pacifism, and the absolute truth of the Lutheran Bible. The Society was dissolved in 1905, and Old Economy Village has been open to the public as a historic site since 1921.

Administered by the Pennsylvania Historical and Museum Commission, Old Economy Village includes fourteen Harmonist buildings, including the hall where feasts were held, the house of founder George Rapp, the Society's store building, and two family dwellings; a large ornamental garden with grotto and pavilion; a graveyard; and an extensive collection of artifacts. Many public programs are sponsored by the Harmonie Associates, Inc., a nonprofit organization.

The Harmony Society *was one of the most successful communal societies in history. Though agriculture was always the basis of the Harmonist economy, it became secondary to their industrial ventures. In later years, the members were supported by paid outside laborers.* OLD ECONOMY VILLAGE

Communal Groups and the Development of the Harmony Society

As long as there have been religions, there have been people who dedicated their lives to worship. Many of these people took their place among the priesthood or the devout, but there were others who entered monasteries or convents, seeking physical as well as spiritual fulfillment. As early as the second century B.C., the Essenes, a Jewish sect, had formed small colonies of worshipers in the wilderness of Palestine. Pre-Christian monks in the Egyptian desert and holy men in Asia retreated from society, believing this would allow them to achieve purity. As Christianity was adopted, some believers formed colonies and sought purity in isolation from the temptations of the world. These people lived under strict sets of rules and rejected most of the practices of the world. No one had property, and they lived in poverty and were celibate. Some individuals, who may or may not have been monks or nuns, isolated themselves as hermits and led ascetic, religious lives.

Others wished to lead a religious life as part of the secular community. They did not want to be monks, but they did not want to live in the world either. This impulse was greatly enhanced by the Protestant Reformation of the sixteenth century, which sought to return Christianity to the pure communities of the early church. Earlier, a Czech reformer, John Huss (1369?–1415), aspired to go back to the fundamental principles of the Bible, have salvation based on belief and good works, reexamine the sacraments, purify the priesthood, and generally reform the Roman Catholic Church. He was executed, but his ideas proved to be very strong. Two broad movements came out of Huss's beliefs: the Moravians, who formed one of the first secular religious communities in the seventeenth century, and the Hutterites, who still have flourishing communities in the Midwest and Canada. These served as a model for later communal societies.

There was a religious upheaval when the Bible was first printed in the 1450s, especially when it was translated and printed in vernacular languages. People reading the newly available Bible found that the biblical churches were not like the highly ritualized medieval church. Early Christian worship was based on belief, not ritual. The sacraments were different, if they existed at all. Baptism was for adults, not children. The first priests were called to their office by a desire to preach, and there was a presumption of their fitness and purity. Ritual was simple, and dogma was reduced to a fervent belief in Jesus Christ. People believing like this tended to form small, intimate congregations, not large religious sects, at least at first.

In sixteenth-century European society, the concept of *country*, or *nation*, was just emerging. Monarchs who wished to extend their authority developed national churches as a way to create what we now call patriotism. To the monarch, dissension from the established church, whether Catholic or Protestant, was viewed as treason and subject to harsh penalties. There were various persecutions, ranging from simple admonitions to fines, or even imprisonment or execution. The New World was seen as a place where the purity of the early church could be recreated. Pennsylvania was one of the few English colonies that offered freedom of religion and thus became a target for early religious communes: Ephrata, in 1735; the Moravians' Bethlehem, in 1741; and the Harmony Society's first community, in 1804. The Shakers were the only early religious organization that did not found its first community in Pennsylvania, but in Watervliet, New York, in 1776.

The communal societies founded in America in the eighteenth and early nineteenth centuries were religious. They were pacifist and often celibate. Beginning in the 1820s, however, there was an explosion of secular communal societies. With some exceptions, these were founded on the principles of either the Scotsman Robert Owen (1771–1856) or the Frenchman Charles Fourier (1772–1837).

Despite a huge body of writings, it is hard to generalize about Owen's ideas.

He was more of a social reformer than a religious visionary. He thought that man was shaped by his environment, and that the ideal environment was a communal society. The community would have a strong intellectual base, own all property, and remedy social ills. The ideas behind the communal society were so self-evident, Owen thought, that once formed, they could only succeed. Owen believed that the architecture of an ideal commune was a single building—thinking influenced by the large textile mills of Great Britain. Such a unitary building would house all the functions of the community, homes, workplaces, schools, barns, and so on. A plan was drawn of such a building. Over time, there were as many as twenty communities that owed some of their ideas to Owen. The heyday of Owenite communities was in the 1820s and 1830s. Although Owen was recognized as a genius (he once addressed the joint houses of Congress), not one of his communities lasted ten years.

Charles Fourier's ideas were not too much different than Owen's. His basic idea was called "joint-stock capitalism." The corporation was already a proven method of doing business. With some adaptations, it would work with communal societies. The community was a large corporation, in which everyone would gather their resources and contribute to the capitalization of the community. Everyone in it would hold stock in the corporation. Self-interest would mean that one would work for the good of the corporation. Since no two people contributed the same amount of capital to the community, stock ownership would contribute some equity. Arguments over who got stock, how much, who could vote (workers or stockholders?), and how many votes each person had were problems of joint-stock communes. Fourier had his communities organized in "Phalanxes," named after the ancient Greek military formations. Fourier's heyday was the 1840s and 1850s. Perhaps there were as many as thirty communities that owed some of their ideas to Fourier.

Fourier was dead by the time his ideas were put to work in America. His ideas were mainly promoted by Albert Brisbane, who was backed by the famous Horace Greeley, publisher of the *New York Tribune*. Greeley actively supported Brisbane and even bought stock in some of the Phalanxes and lived in one for a short time.

There were other types of communal groups as well. Most communal societies developed in open land, but a few formed in cities, figuring there would be more work for their members there. The famous Brook Farm, which started as a Fourierite Society, was supported more by donations than by any communal effort. It became a center for intellectuals in New England, and this far outweighed its importance as a commune.

In general, religious communities lasted longer than secular ones; celibate communities lasted longer than noncelibate, perhaps because leaders were able to concentrate their members' efforts more narrowly. The Shakers have been in existence since 1774. The Harmony Society lasted 120 years, from 1785 to 1905. It is estimated that some 200,000 people participated in about 190 communal societies before 1900. Their contribution to American industry and intellectual thought, to say nothing of the religious freedom they enjoyed, far outweighed their small numbers. There still are several communal societies today, mostly in the midwestern states and western Canada.

George Rapp, founder of the Harmony Society, served as its leader for more than forty years. OLD ECONOMY VILLAGE

GEORGE RAPP AND HIS FOLLOWERS

The founder of the Harmony Society, George Rapp, was born Johannes Georg Rapp in 1757 in Iptingen, Württemberg, the southwestern part of what is today Germany. He came from a family of sturdy farmers and received an education in the town school, learning to read and write in the local Swabian dialect. He was evidently trained as a vinedresser and linen weaver. In 1783, he married Christina Benzinger and later had a son, Johannes, and a daughter, Rosina. In his twenties, Rapp had little to do during an illness but read the Bible. During this enforced idleness, he experienced a religious awakening and felt the call to preach. He began holding services and gathered many followers. Among them was a man named Frederick Reichert (1775–1834), whom Rapp later adopted as a son. Before long, Rapp's followers ceased their attendance at the local Lutheran church and stopped observing some of the sacraments.

In 1787, Rapp formed a pietistic congregation. Little is known about this group in Germany, but Rapp claimed he had ten thousand followers at one time. Whether he had that many or not, he had enough of a following to cause the local church-state authorities some alarm. Rapp never strayed very far from the Lutheran beliefs of Württemberg, but he did not follow their form of worship. The Lutheran Church investigated him on several occasions and he was imprisoned. Before one of the synod trials he declared: "I am a prophet and called to be one."

Ludwig, duke of Württemberg, and the Lutheran Synod of Maulbronn, did not want any religious controversy and tried to keep things calm. The pastor of Iptingen was told to handle Rapp "with love and gentleness," something he was not able to do. Though Rapp was jailed for a time and forbidden to preach, he continued anyway.

THE MOVE TO AMERICA AND THE FIRST SETTLEMENT

Although active religious persecution was only occasional, and not very onerous, Rapp decided to emigrate with his followers. In 1802, on behalf of the Harmony Society, Rapp petitioned Napoleon for land in French Louisiana. The following year, he was instead offered a tract in the Pyrenees, because the United States had purchased Louisiana in 1803. The land in the Pyre-

nees was not satisfactory. After briefly considering the idea of settling in what is now the Czech Republic, Rapp decided to move to America, which had a reputation in Europe as being the Promised Land. There was a lull in the Napoleonic Wars in 1803, and Rapp and a small advance party embarked on a ship from Holland to America, leaving his followers behind under the leadership of Frederick Reichert Rapp. The party landed in Philadelphia, where the local German community welcomed them, and before long, George Rapp began preaching in the German churches of Philadelphia and Lancaster. In 1804, the balance of the followers, organized by Frederick Rapp, had come to America. Some of the new arrivals went off on their own, leaving Rapp with about five hundred followers.

Rapp had spent a considerable amount of time looking for land, and on July 12, 1804, he talked to President Thomas Jefferson in Washington about a government land grant in the Louisiana Purchase territory. Later that year, however, Rapp and his followers bought about four thousand acres in Butler County in western Pennsylvania, where they began to build the town of Harmony. *Harmonie* was a term used by Pietists for the kind of religious discipline they practiced—to live in peace and harmony with oneself, one's fellow man, and one's God.

The settlers first constructed log buildings, and later built permanent dwellings of frame or brick. Their original intention was to build a farming community much like the small towns they had known in Germany. Their largest building was a granary, used to store grain in preparation for the prophesied Millennium, similar to the public granaries back in their homeland. They did well at first selling farm products.

One of the first things the settlers built was a small fulling mill to finish local weavers' broadcloth—a small beginning of what was to become a huge textile business at later settlements.

By 1807, they were sufficiently established to start building brick structures around a small central square. George Rapp designed the town, influenced by the vernacular architecture of eastern Pennsylvania. Today, visitors to the town of Harmony can see domestic, farm, and commercial buildings.

THE FORMATION OF THE HARMONY SOCIETY

In 1805, the newly arrived followers of George Rapp formed a communal society, George Rapp and Associates, known as the Harmony Society. The members signed a covenant giving all their property to the Society. (They could draw it out if they left, but this option was withdrawn later.) In return, the Society agreed to supply all the necessities of life—shelter, food, clothing, education— and religious instruction. Both men and women signed the Articles of Agreement, which was a secular contract rather than a set of religious beliefs, though everything they did had a religious purpose. This covenant lasted until 1816, when a new one was created transferring all property rights to the Society. The book recording the amounts of donated property was burned, putting all members on an equal footing.

In 1807, the Society experienced a deep religious enlightenment. As a result, they adopted celibacy as a practice, which was enforced by Rapp and adhered to by most members. After 1831, the rule on celibacy became more strictly enforced, but a new child was born into

CHRONOLOGY

1757 George Rapp born

1785 Harmony Society formed as a religious organization in Germany

1803 First migration of Harmonists to United States takes place

1804 Harmony, Pennsylvania, settled

1805 Harmony Society formed as a communal society

1807 Celibacy adopted

1814 The Society buys the site for Harmony, Indiana

1815 Harmonists move to Harmony, Indiana, and sell old site to a Mennonite congregation

1824 Frederick Rapp buys the site for Economy, Pennsylvania

1825 Harmonists move to Economy and sell Harmony, Indiana, to Robert Owen

1832 Schism in which one-third of members leave to follow Count de Leon

1847 George Rapp dies on August 7 and R. L. Baker becomes senior trustee

1868 Baker dies and Jacob Henrici becomes senior trustee

1892 Henrici dies and John Duss becomes senior trustee

1903 Duss resigns and wife Susie Creese Duss becomes senior trustee

1905 Society is dissolved by Susie Duss

1916 Remaining property is secured by Commonwealth of Pennsylvania

1919 Pennsylvania Historical Commission assumes responsibility for site

1921 Site is opened as a museum

1951 John Duss dies

THE HARMONY SOCIETY AND SILK

During the 1820s and 1830s, an enthusiasm for silk swept America. As part of this trend, the Harmonists began their silk production in 1826. The silkworm makes a cocoon of a single strand of silk. Separating the silk fiber is a very difficult task. The worm has to be killed and the cocoon steamed to dissolve the binder that holds the thread together. Then one has to find the end of the strand and unwind it. A single strand is too fine to use alone, so several have to be twisted together to make a useful thread. The threads are then dyed and woven into cloth. The fineness of the thread makes this all very difficult. Producing silk cloth is very time-consuming, and it turned out to be an almost impossible job for the Harmonists to make silk cloth that could be sold at a reasonable price. For their production, the Society grew about one million cocoons, so theirs was no small production. For a time, the U.S. government paid a subsidy on cocoons, but this was not enough to make it worthwhile.

Silkworms are very particular as to what they eat and will only eat mulberry leaves, which are not native to North America. Cuttings, therefore, had to be imported from France and Italy. The Harmonists eventually had about ten acres of mulberry trees. As part of their nursery tree business, they made money selling mulberry cuttings to other silk growers. One can still find white mulberries growing wild near the site grounds.

Initially under George Rapp's supervision, Gertrude Rapp, George's granddaughter, became an expert in silk production and was consulted by other silk weavers. The Harmonists had trouble unwinding the threads, so instead, they at first chopped it into small pieces and spun it as if it were tow (short pieces of flax).

The Harmonists made material for men's vests, lustings (cloth that was chemically treated to make it shine), handkerchiefs, cravats, satin, velvet, and sewing thread. In 1839, Gertrude Rapp received a gold medal from the American Institute's New York exhibition for the "best specimens of silk velvets and fancy ribbons." In 1844, she received first place medals for silk fabrics in New York, Boston, and Philadelphia. Previously, in 1841, George Rapp presented President John Tyler with enough material to make a suit. That same year, the Society had so much unsold silk cloth that it gave every member enough silk to make a Sunday dress suit of clothes. A year's production yielded less than $2,000, however, so it was never profitable. The Harmonists still occasionally made silk but discontinued production by 1844.

The museum has several medals and many examples of silk of Harmony Society manufacture, including numerous sets of the Sunday clothes the Harmonists wore.

Silk Exhibit. The Harmonist Society entered this display of silk in the Women's Pavilion at the Columbian Exposition of 1892 in Chicago.

the Society nearly every year. There were a few marriages performed while the group resided in Harmony, but even fewer later. One of the marriages was that of Rapp's son, John, in 1807. Out of that union a daughter, Gertrude, was born. In the celibate households, husbands and wives lived together as brothers and sisters, adapting their living arrangements to accommodate their new practice.

THE HARMONY SOCIETY AS A MANUFACTURING ORGANIZATION

The American colonies did very little manufacturing, but after the Revolution, efforts were made to foster American industry and decrease the reliance on imported European goods. Industrial development was sluggish at first, because European imports, chiefly British, were cheap and prevalent. Beginning in the 1790s, however, the United States began to emerge as an industrial presence. In the early nineteenth century, American manufacturing was strengthened as a consequence of the Napoleonic Wars, which effectively cut off several European markets, and by America's withdrawal from the British market, which resulted after political protest against British maritime policies. By the 1840s, domestic products were plentiful, reliance on European imports was at a minimum, and the country was fully immersed in the Industrial Revolution. The Harmony Society was part of this process, and in industries such as silk manufacturing, it was considered a leader.

The Society became a successful manufacturer of textiles while in Harmony, Pennsylvania. Frederick Rapp bought merino sheep to upgrade the Society's flocks. The wool was of higher quality and production doubled. The Society built a carding and woolen mill and started producing broadcloth and flannels. It also went into the production of cotton sheeting and linen cloth and produced hemp for rope and cloth, as well as cotton yarn for local weavers. The Society's products were sold in Pittsburgh and the upper Ohio Valley, and it even shipped some of its better-quality goods to Baltimore and Philadelphia. In 1811, a traveler saw about 450 pieces of cloth in the Society's warehouse. This much cloth would have required over ten tons of wool, and this was only one year's production. The Society only produced about two and a half tons from its own flock, so it had to buy wool from local farmers, who, in turn, bought Harmonist goods. The Society produced a cash surplus as their income went up dramatically.

THE MOVE TO INDIANA

In 1814, the Harmonists purchased about 3,560 acres in southern Indiana and across the Wabash River in Illinois Territory. They built a second town, also called Harmony, and sold old Harmony to a group of Mennonites. Although the publicly stated reason for moving to Indiana was that the Society needed land for sheep, the real reason was that it wanted to build a manufacturing town and control enough land to be isolated from and independent of the world. It therefore needed more land for expansion and better access to a water supply and river transportation. The Society eventually acquired more than twenty thousand acres. Frederick Rapp made architectural recommendations to George Rapp, who led a team to Indiana to build the new town in the wilderness. The new town's large cruciform church, derived from one of Father Rapp's visions, could hold most of the members. Four large dormitories for unmarried young people were built on the order of boardinghouses in eastern textile towns.

HARMONIST DRESS

The Harmonists did not have a dress code. As in modern communal societies, there was a range of acceptable dress styles. Uniformity arose because most of the clothing was made by a small group of people. The Society's tailor made the men's clothing. The women's clothing was made by a group of seamstresses. Some clothing, however, was made in the home. The styles were based on those brought from Germany, modified by the American experience. Until the 1830s, no one had commented on Harmonist dress, so it may not have varied too much from American styles of the time. Later, more people began to notice the peculiar dress, so the early-nineteenth-century styles must have remained fixed in Harmonist society.

Colors were mainly dark blue with some brown for ordinary wear. The Harmonists used woad, a common weed, for their blue dye, but they were experts with indigo as well.

The women dressed in bell-shaped skirts that almost touched the ground, often made with six or eight panels. There were no hoops, bustles, or flounces to bell the skirt out. They wore fitted bodices with high necks and long sleeves. For formal dress, the women wore peaked hats made up of thick ribs. For ordinary wear, women's hats were very plain. In the summer, the women who worked outdoors wore wide straw hats to shade their faces.

Women also wore aprons of white unbleached cotton or linen for everyday wear. Black silk aprons with deep, ironed creases were worn on Sundays. The aprons did not have bibs. The women wore scarves over their shoulders with the ends tucked in their aprons' waist straps. These scarves were plain. At least after 1842, however, there was a style for Sunday wear made out of blue silk.

At the end of the Napoleonic Wars, there was a lot of unrest in Europe. In 1817, the Society sent representatives to Germany to recruit new members. The effort was a success. The Society grew to nearly nine hundred members during this period, despite a death toll from frequent outbreaks of malaria. Many of the new members, however, were not as committed as the original members, and few stayed with the Society for very long.

One of the greatest desires of farmers at this time was to find a cash product.

The Harmonists probably tried many different products, but they found only one that brought in money consistently: cloth, both woolen and cotton. Cloth was easier to ship to market than farm goods, and it had a ready market on the frontier. Frederick Rapp built steam-powered cotton and woolen mills in New Harmony. For a brief period, the Society held the U.S. production record for cotton sheeting. But the Harmonists consistently had trouble finding sufficient raw wool in southern Indiana. They

Men wore surtouts, which are loose jackets with sleeves about fingertip length. A contemporary photograph of one shows a collar, but earlier versions may not have had one. These were worn over white shirts. For Sunday, men wore frock coats that were tightly fitted to the body but with flaring skirts that came below the knees. Men wore vests under these. After 1841, men's Sunday clothing was made of blue silk. The examples of trousers that survive were worn high at the waist and were supported by

suspenders. They have button flies but earlier versions must have had fall-front flaps, similar to what modern Amish or Old Order Mennonites wear. The men also wore Harmonist-made hats in various styles. Most had fairly wide brims and creased crowns. For Sunday dress, men wore the tall top hats that were popular in the nineteenth century.

Both sexes wore high shoes, but men who worked outdoors had boots. There are numerous examples of Harmonist clothing in the collection of Old Economy Village.

eventually found supplies in the hills of Kentucky, where they often dealt with the Shakers, another communal group.

As there were no large population centers near Harmony, Indiana, the Society built small retail stores in three Indiana towns, reselling goods purchased in Philadelphia and New Orleans. The Society hired nonmembers to run the stores and also wholesaled goods to independent merchants. This method was more complicated and less profitable, but the Society still prospered.

The Society's neighbors did not know how to live with a religious communal society, and there was tension between them. The Harmonists tended to vote in a bloc for conservative candidates— something that did not go over well with the freewheeling frontiersmen. Despite this, Frederick Rapp was active in the Whig party and served in the territorial legislature. He was on the committee that picked the location of the new state capital of Indianapolis and submitted the design for the first state capitol building.

History of Old Economy Village

However well the Harmonists prospered in Indiana, they were too far from the sources of supply for raw wool and markets for the finished cloth. On a trip to Philadelphia in 1824, Frederick Rapp found that there was a block of about six hundred acres for sale at a place called Dead Man's Ripple, on the east bank of the Ohio River, just eighteen miles north of Pittsburgh in Beaver County. He bought the land and, after drawing a map of the proposed town and setting out markers for George Rapp's consideration, he returned to Indiana. There he organized a crew of craftsmen for Father Rapp to take back to start building the new town. This tract of land was only seven square miles, a lot smaller than what the Harmonists owned in Indiana. They planned to give up large-scale farming and build a manufacturing town.

They called their new town Oekonomie (Economy), meaning "a place of orderly, managed affairs." This is a term used by pietistic societies for the "divine economy" that they hoped to establish on earth—that is, a Christian, communal, pacifistic society.

The first members transferred to the new town were the craftsmen and builders. By the spring of 1825, they had put up enough buildings to house everyone, so the rest of the community moved to Economy.

In 1824, the society had begun advertising to find a buyer for its land in Indiana but had little luck until Robert Owen, a Scottish industrialist who had made his money in textiles and wanted to establish a secular communal society, became interested. Owen bought the land and renamed the town New Harmony, but his experiment lasted less than two years. However, New Harmony continued to attract intellectuals and scientists, who discovered and classified many of the natural wonders of the West. Several of the buildings of the Harmony Society still stand.

The Harmonists quickly built the new community of Economy. As the new town was to be a manufacturing community, not a farming one, they

The Harmonist Church. Religion was at the center of all Harmonist activity. The church building at Economy was completed in 1832. OLD ECONOMY VILLAGE

Economy, Rapp's Colony on the Ohio, *1832*. *A Swiss artist, Karl Bodmer (1809–93), painted this watercolor of Economy in its early years.* JOSLYN ART MUSEUM, OMAHA, NEBRASKA (EA42)

rushed to get their store open, which they did in 1825. They moved a year's supply of cloth to the new community so they would have something to sell while they built their new factories. They then built their cotton and woolen mills, so they could start bringing in money. As they had done in their other communities, they laid the town out in a grid, but this time without a central square.

This manufacturing town was divided into quarters. The northwest quarter held the tannery, flour mill, and steam-powered woolen mill; the southwest, the cotton mill; the southeast, the barns for cattle and horses; and the northeast, the silk mill, pigs, and the laundry. The Harmonists built 119 family-size houses, eighty of which still stand. As in their other communities, the first houses were built of logs on the backs of lots to provide temporary housing for the workers until more permanent buildings could be constructed on the streets. One of these log structures

still exists on 15th Street, just north of the historic site in modern Ambridge.

The community was a private, isolated world for the members of the Society, but there was a business area along Main Street, which is now 14th Street. On this street were the hotel where outsiders could stay and the large building that housed the Society's museum and its feast hall, where the religious festivals were observed. George and Frederick Rapp's first houses were on Main Street, as was the storekeeper's house and Store, which functioned as both an outlet for the community's manufactured goods and a general retail store for the neighbors in the surrounding community. At the Store, farmers could barter their wool for manufactured goods or purchase them with money or bills of credit. By 1826, the village had its own post office. As was common in the period, it was located in the Store. Farther along was the Mechanics Building, where shoes were made and repaired. It also held the

The Feast Hall/Museum Building was where the community held their Love Feasts and exhibited their extensive natural history and art collections. OLD ECONOMY VILLAGE

tailor shop and some hat-making operations. If the public wanted to do business with the Harmony Society, it was all within this two-block area.

The town had its own running water supply, which was piped from springs above the village to the east. They had a community fire department complete with a Harmonist-produced fire engine. Each floor of the factories held a water tank in case of fire. This was all very progressive for the time. The Society even put the steamboat it had built for the move from New Harmony, the *William Penn*, to use as a packet boat, hauling passengers and freight between Pitts-

"A Place of Orderly Managed Affairs." *The people of Economy sought to build an American Utopia. This view was photographed around 1890.* OLD ECONOMY VILLAGE

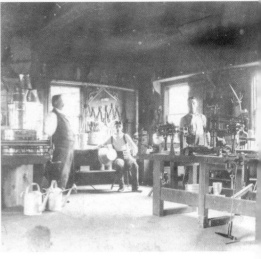

Harmonist Industry. Two examples of Harmonist industrial enterprise were captured in these c. 1890 photographs of the lumber works and the tin shop. OLD ECONOMY VILLAGE

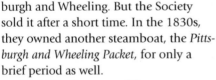

burgh and Wheeling. But the Society sold it after a short time. In the 1830s, they owned another steamboat, the *Pittsburgh and Wheeling Packet*, for only a brief period as well.

By 1831, the town of Economy was well established. The members were all housed in substantial dwellings. They were supplied with good provisions in abundant quantity. They had a functioning water system. Their mills were producing ample cloth that had a wide market. There were schools for children and adults, as well as a band, museum, deer park, and botanical garden. The Society was prosperous and everything appeared to be well.

THE SCHISM

In 1830, the Society had about five hundred members. However, many of them had joined after the Napoleonic Wars or were children of the founders and did not have the same motivation of the original members. They had not been persecuted in Württemberg or forced to make the difficult voyage to America and build the original settlements in the wilderness. Rapp felt that the new mem-

bers wanted the rewards of their predecessors' work.

In the midst of this, Rapp had received correspondence from a man titling himself as "Count de Leon, the Lion of Judah," but whose real name was Bernard Proli. Leon proclaimed himself the Messiah to Rapp. Apparently, as Rapp was expecting the Messiah in 1829, he was willing to recognize Leon as such, if only for a very short period of time. Leon arrived at Economy in 1831 with his entourage, and they were lodged in the hotel and later in family houses. Leon was also provided with a laboratory for his alchemy experiments. Rapp's rapport with Leon did not last through their first meeting.

During the winter, however, a number of younger Harmonists rallied around Leon when he promised a community without celibacy. By spring, a full-fledged schism had developed. About 170 of Rapp's followers—one-third of the members—joined with Leon and left the Society. They demanded their share of the Society's assets. The various agreements that members had signed did not allow for this, but in

1832, the Society made a settlement with the "Seceders," as they were called, and eventually gave them $250,000. The Society was low on cash and had to call on their debtors to raise the money. The handling of the third payment was bungled so badly that the Seceders rioted and the militia had to be called out to drive them away. The ex-members later built the town of Phillipsburgh, now Monaca, Pennsylvania, downstream on the Ohio River, just opposite the Beaver River.

Leon moved on and later founded another community at Grand Ecore, Louisiana, called Germantown. Other former Harmonists later joined with Dr. William Keil, another Utopian, at Bethel, Missouri. In 1855, some of Keil's people moved to communities in Zoar, Ohio, and Aurora, Oregon. One former Harmonist, Jacob Zundel, joined the Mormons and migrated with them to Utah.

As part of the negotiations with the Seceders, the Society had appointed two trustees and a council of fifteen heads of shops, all reporting to George Rapp. With Father Rapp so active, however, these officials were merely advisory. They met weekly to discuss business and set schedules during Rapp's tenure. But this governmental structure was to prove more valuable later.

In 1833, the woolen mill burned down. The Society blamed this on the Seceders, but fires were common in textile mills, so it is uncertain what caused it. By the following year, the Society had a new mill in operation.

As a result of the schism, George Rapp resolved never to be caught short of funds again. Over the next few years, he built up a "church fund" of $510,000 in gold and silver coins, which he kept in a vault under the floor of his office. The funds were later used to buy an operating interest in the Pittsburgh and Lake Erie (P&LE) Railroad, with Jacob Henrici as president.

The Harmonist Hotel housed Count de Leon and his entourage when they arrived in 1831.
OLD ECONOMY VILLAGE

HOW THE HARMONY SOCIETY
WAS GOVERNED

How does one govern an organization that sets up a heaven on earth? A lot like one governs a secular community. The Harmony Society consisted of followers of George Rapp. There was little doubt that he was in charge. Everything in the community had his stamp, but he was not an absolute ruler. There was a second string under him who had a great deal of independence in their fields of expertise. Frederick Rapp handled the day-to-day business, and the Langenbachers (Bakers) ran the Store. Each foreman was in charge of his own craft shop. Sunday afternoons the foremen met to discuss the Society's business and decide upon a schedule for the week. Under these conditions, it would be an insensitive leader indeed who did not know what his community was thinking. For example, the idea to adopt celibacy came from the members, not Rapp.

Once a year, the Harmonists held a sort of annual meeting. All the branches of the Society would report, and when their accounts were approved, their books were taken out in front of the church building and burned.

Following the schism and Frederick Rapp's death, George Rapp assumed the Society's secular functions but delegated the day-to-day business. Two trustees and a council of elders were appointed. After Father Rapp's death, the Senior Trustee, R. L. Baker, took charge, assuming all of Rapp's powers. The Junior Trustee, Jacob Henrici, had some power, but it was subject to the Society and Baker. Henrici became Senior Trustee upon Baker's death. John S. Duss later became the Junior Trustee. Then, when Henrici died, Duss became the head of the Society. During Duss's reign, the elders met occasionally to rubber-stamp his decisions.

ECONOMY'S ZENITH

Before the schism, the Harmony Society had been economically open to the outside world. The Harmonists had a printing press on which they printed their hymnbook and some thoughts of George Rapp. Later, *Thoughts on the Destiny of Man* (1824) was translated into English and printed on their press in Indiana. They had a small orchestra and gave concerts for Society members and invited guests. All this ended after the schism. Except for their businesses, the Society withdrew from the world. The people who left in the schism tended to be the younger and newer members. The Harmonists managed to keep their mills going, but the concerts and most other attempts to open the Society to the world were ended.

In 1834, Frederick Rapp, who had been the head of the Harmonists' business interests, the architect, and the foremost spokesman for the Society, died. All of the Society's property had been held in his name. George Rapp assumed the business interests of the Society and had all the property placed in his name. For a while everything went on as before. Then, in 1837, there was a depression, just at the time the Harmonists would have updated and reequipped all their textile mills. With the depression in full force, they were unable to make the renovations, and the textile manufacturing slowed down significantly. By the mid-1840s, the Harmonists made very little cloth, although they never completely stopped making it. (In 1875, a traveler saw webs still in the looms.) By 1850, however, the cloth mills were essentially closed down. The Society's principal business activity now was fattening cattle for market. This was all a prelude to a huge spurt of economic growth, but for a while the pace slowed.

In 1847, George Rapp died. The *Pittsburgh Daily Morning Post* called him "the greatest communist of the age." Rapp's death stunned the Society, but life went on. The future, however, would be different.

GEORGE RAPP'S SUCCESSORS

The two trustees—R. L. Baker (Gottlieb Romelius Langenbacher, 1793–1868) and Jacob Henrici (1804-92)—began managing the affairs of the Society. Although technically both trustees ruled, in actual practice the one in charge was the Senior Trustee, R. L. Baker. Baker's father had been the first storekeeper for the Society, and his oldest son, John L. Baker (born 1782), had been after him. John died in 1825, and R. L. became the

Jacob Henrici, George Rapp's faithful assistant, assumed the position of Senior Trustee in 1868, after the death of R. L. Baker.

OLD ECONOMY VILLAGE

storekeeper and then business agent in his brother's place. Coming from a family of storekeepers, Baker learned to speak and write English well enough to act as the translator for the Society. As trustee, he first continued the practices of George Rapp. With all their capital and knowledge of manufacturing and merchandising, it was not long before the Society expanded their capitalist ventures, only this time it was away from Economy and using outside agents. Jacob Henrici became Senior Trustee when Baker died in 1868. A Bavarian, Henrici joined the Harmony Society in 1826. He was the schoolmaster for a while but, by 1831, had become George Rapp's assistant and was living in Rapp's house. In his own way, Henrici was as great a visionary leader as George or Frederick Rapp.

THE HARMONY SOCIETY AS A CAPITALIST INVESTOR

The Harmonists were pioneers of the oil business. This venture began when they loaned money to the proprietor of a small tract of land adjacent to their lumber farm in Warren County, Pennsylvania. The borrower, however, was unable to repay the loan, so the Society secured the land as payment for the debt. Shortly after, Edwin L. Drake started drilling for oil on nearby land. He brought in the first oil well in 1859, near Titusville. The Harmonists struck oil the following year and entrusted the former proprietor with the management of the land. The Harmonists had been drilling on their land prior to this, most likely for water to supply the steam engine in their lumbermill. In this area, water wells were frequently fouled by oil. The Society entered the oil business under the name of the Economy Oil Company, which they eventually sold out to the Rockefeller interests.

The Harmonists occasionally hired non-Society workers who lived in the community. One such person was John Fox, an Englishman, who resided in the hotel in the late 1820s while he built a Jacquard loom for the silk mill. By the 1860s, most of the members were elderly and there were not enough workers, so the Society started to bring in more paid workers. These were mainly German-speaking immigrants, whom the Society provided with housing, food, and clothing. At first, the Society dressed these paid workers in Harmonist clothing, at least for Sunday wear, and treated them more or less as members. Later, the paid workers were clothed like other Americans. The paid workers did not practice celibacy. By the late 1880s, almost all agricultural and other heavy work done in the community was by paid workers.

In 1868, the Harmonists bought and developed the site of the town of Beaver Falls, Pennsylvania, for its position on the falls of the Beaver River. Water power to run the mills was very important before electricity was available. They sold some of the land for the town and donated the land upon which Geneva College now stands but kept a number of existing manufacturing sites, including a cutlery company and a ceramics company, and acquired a file-making company. They eventually sold the file company to the Nicholson File Company and the ceramics company to the Mayer Brothers. The ceramics company later became part of what is now Syracuse China Company. The Society employed Chinese labor in the cutlery company, a revolutionary concept for western Pennsylvania. Typical of the Harmonists, they built the Chinese workers a church. They also founded the Economy Bank, which funded the businesses of the new town.

The Harmonists acquired interests in five railroads. Their biggest holding was

Oil. *The Harmonists struck oil at Economy in 1860, a year after Edwin Drake in Titusville, and added the oil industry to their roster of business ventures. To the right is an oil derrick. The two large structures to the left are charcoal ovens.* OLD ECONOMY VILLAGE

now became Senior Trustee and head of the Society. Duss always claimed that the Society was in dire financial straits when he took over, but it is difficult to uncover the real circumstances. Whatever the truth may be, Duss liquidated the overextended Economy Bank, as well as other external holdings of the Society. He sold the portion of Economy surrounding the historic hub to the Berlin Iron Works for $4 million. Berlin later became the American Bridge Company, which later became part of U.S. Steel. American Bridge renamed the town after itself, Ambridge, in 1902. In 1903, Susie C. Duss (1859–1946) became the last trustee, as her husband John withdrew

in the Pittsburgh and Lake Erie Railroad, in which they had an operating interest. To buy the common stock, they used the church fund of $510,000 that George Rapp had built up after the schism, though they used other capital as well. The money had been kept in a damp vault and was tarnished. Supposedly, a few of the more trusted members took all the coins and shined them up before the purchase. The boards used to hold the coins for shining are still in Old Economy's collection. Jacob Henrici was president of the railroad for five years. After his death, most of the Society's invested interests were sold.

THE END OF THE HARMONY SOCIETY

Jacob Henrici died on Christmas Day in 1892. He was the last of the members who had helped build the town of Economy. The number of members had dwindled to six. John S. Duss (1860–1951), a former schoolteacher who had been the Junior Trustee under Henrici,

John S. Duss led the Society in its declining years. OLD ECONOMY VILLAGE

25

Historic Site. Old Economy Village was the state's first historic site, acquired in 1918.

In 1903, using Society funds, Duss hired the Metropolitan Opera Orchestra and set up a Venetian canal in Madison Square Garden, New York, complete with gondolas for the performances. He went on a national tour of the United States. Duss equated himself with John Philip Sousa, but the critics were less kind. The concerts ended in 1903, though the Economy Band continued to exist through 1905.

OLD ECONOMY VILLAGE IN RECENT YEARS

The Commonwealth of Pennsylvania tried to assume title to the remaining assets of the Society on the grounds that there were no longer any members or heirs and that the organization had ceased to exist. The few remaining buildings and six acres of land were turned over to the state in 1916. The commonwealth took title to the property but the court allowed the monetary assets and collections of the Society to remain in the hands of John and Susie Duss.

From 1916 to 1921, what is now Old Economy Village was dormant. It was placed under the care of the Pennsylvania Historical Commission, now the Pennsylvania Historical and Museum Commission (PHMC), in 1918. In 1921, local citizens formed the Harmonist Historical and Memorial Association to care for the site, and the Historical Commission subsequently turned the operation of the site over to them. This was one of the first historic villages open to the public in the country, ahead of Williamsburg by five years, and it was the Historical Commission's first historic site. The collection of the Society, including furniture, tools, cloth-

as a member, and she dissolved the Society in 1905. But this was not the end.

Although John Duss claimed in his book, *The Harmonists,* that when he assumed leadership the Society was completely without funds, there were still plenty of assets. In 1890, Duss had reorganized the Economy Band and had been giving performances. By 1899, he had given public performances in Pittsburgh, Wheeling, and other nearby towns, with himself as the conductor.

OTHER RELATED SITES

THE CHURCH

Outside the historic site is the Harmonist Church, which was completed in 1832. Typical of churches of the period, its exterior is oriented toward the east. Atypically, the Harmonists oriented their service to the south side of the building, with George Rapp preaching his sermons from a small, raised platform under the arched window. The men sat on his right and the women sat on his left; there were separate doors for men and women.

The church is now St. John's Lutheran Church. The original Harmonist pews are still in use today. The Harmonist-made clock with three one-handed faces is still in the tower. A bell tolls each quarter hour. The steeple is topped with a cross and chanticleer, or rooster.

THE CEMETERY

Three blocks south on Church Street is the Harmonist Cemetery, which was originally within the apple orchard. The Harmonists did not believe in memorializing members and did not use tombstones, so the place appears to be a bare field except for a few small tombstones, which were for paid workers or married members of the Society. Most have initials rather than names. About 350 Harmonists are buried here. This location was chosen for the Cemetery because there was a small Indian mound there with several burials. The mound

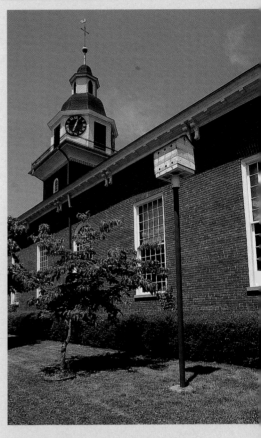

was removed after 1902 to make space for building sites and the American Bridge Company bridge.

ing, and the archives, remained the property of the Dusses until 1938. In that year, the Historical Commission began operation of the site, and the WPA Writers' Project started working on the collection and developed a catalog. This project ended in 1942. In 1961, funds were appropriated to restore the village. It was closed from 1961 to 1965 for restoration but has been operated as a historic site ever since. Restoration and development of the site continue today. The most recent additions are the new Visitor Center and the recreated natural history and fine arts museum in the Feast Hall/Museum Building.

Visiting the Site

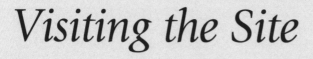

PA Route 65

15B

15A

15

13th Street

Greenhouse

16A

SITE LEGEND

1	Visitor Center	**12**	The Lenz House*
2	The Feast Hall/Museum Building	**13**	The Store and Post Office
3	The Community Kitchen	**14**	The Mechanics Building and Wine Cellar
4	The Cabinet Shop	**15**	George Rapp Garden
5	The Granary	**15A**	Pavilion
6	Bake Oven	**15B**	Grotto
7	Warehouse	**16**	The George Rapp House
8	Pump		
9	The Baker House	**16A**	Carriage House
10	Baker House Garden	**17**	The Frederick Rapp House
11	Family Shed		Restrooms

* Not open to the public

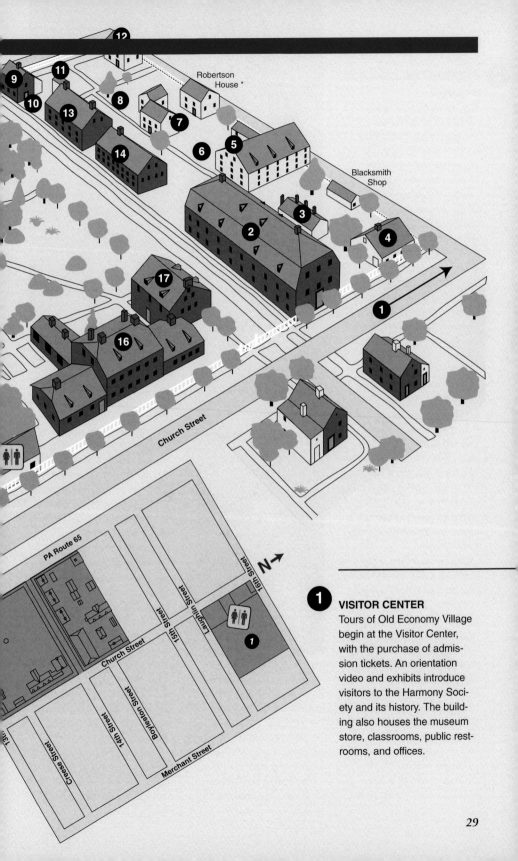

Robertson House *

Blacksmith Shop

Church Street

PA Route 65

Church Street

Merchant Street

VISITOR CENTER
Tours of Old Economy Village begin at the Visitor Center, with the purchase of admission tickets. An orientation video and exhibits introduce visitors to the Harmony Society and its history. The building also houses the museum store, classrooms, public restrooms, and offices.

2 THE FEAST HALL/MUSEUM BUILDING

The Harmonists held feasts about four times a year, though in some years they had as many as seven or eight. The Love Feast, or *Liebesmahl*, was a common practice in pietistic societies. When George Rapp was preaching in Germany, the Harmonists held a Love Feast every week. In America, the Society had feasts on the anniversary of the Society's founding (February 15), Easter, Christmas, Harvest Home (a thanksgiving festival usually held in August), and when the mood struck them. Later, they also had one on the anniversary of George Rapp's death, August 7. When they had problems, such as during the schism, they often had additional Love Feasts, as many as three in one week. The feast included a meal and a religious service and lasted all day. The Harmonists also held a commemoration of the Last Supper here each year before Easter.

Little is known about how the Love Feast was conducted, as outsiders were never invited. Prior to the feast, the members would confess all individual differences before Father Rapp. If their feast was conducted like those of other pietistic societies, it would have included the ritual of participants giving each other the "kiss of peace" on the cheek. Once all were in "the harmony," they would go into the feast.

Until the schism of 1832, the Society had no building in which they could assemble

all the members at one time. When the Feast Hall was built in 1826, it could hold only half the members. In the summer, the Society could hold its feasts outdoors, but many of its feasts were held in cold weather.

The exterior architecture is similar to large public buildings in Germany. It is a two-story building with a hipped roof. Typical of such buildings, it has a number of rooms on the first floor and a large meeting hall on the second. The vaulted meeting room, or *Saal* (opposite page top), is fifty-two by one hundred feet in size. An arched ceiling was also used in the wine cellar and the Harmonist church. The room has been painted only twice in its 175-year history, and the present colors are based on historic paint analysis. Although visitors see only the west staircase, there is a similar one at the east end. The Harmonists segregated their members by sex, and one staircase was for the women and the other was for the men. The central doors above the entrances are a mystery. Their use is unknown. George Rapp may have deliv-

ered sermons or read poetry on special occasions from the door at the west end. There are similar doors in the Harmonist church building and in the church where Rapp worshiped in Iptingen.

On the first floor, the Harmonists established a natural history and fine arts museum. Also on this floor were a classroom, manager's office, and music practice room. The museum was built by the community's first doctor, Johannes Christoph Müller (1752–1845). As a trained medical doctor, Müller, along with Frederick Rapp, was one of the intellectuals of the Society. At Economy, he had a herbarium, was a schoolteacher, led the orchestra, and managed the museum, gathering and preserving local specimens for the collection. In 1826, the Society had bought objects from collectors and dealers, building up a sizable collection of natural history and mineral specimens, as well as a large art collection. Remaining in the collections are a static electricity machine and some microscopes, the premier scientific instruments of their day. The museum was opened

to the public in 1827. As Müller left in the schism of 1832, the succeeding doctor, Conrad Feucht, became the museum manager. After Frederick Rapp's death in 1834, George Rapp put the entire museum up for sale. He offered it to the scientists of New Harmony, but they were not interested. Much of the mineral collection was sold to what is now the University of Pittsburgh in 1852. Before 1892, a microscope was given by Jacob Henrici to the museum that in 1896 became Carnegie Museum. The microscope had initially been owned by Carolus Linnaeus (1707–78), the Swedish botanist who developed the present system of taxonomy.

The Harmony Society held classes for adult members. These were mainly on religious subjects, but there also were classes on drawing or art, physics, astronomy, chemistry, and natural history. The southwest room in the Feast Hall/Museum Building was used as a classroom.

Most of the buildings, including this one, have grapevines growing on trellises on the east, south, and west sides—a

practice brought from Europe. The bricks would help warm the grapes in the fall and the grapeleaves cooled the walls in the summer. This effect worked on wooden buildings as well. The Harmonists made large quantities of wine, which were stored in a large wine cellar under the west end of the building, as well as in the arched wine cellar beneath the Mechanics Building.

3 **THE COMMUNITY KITCHEN**

The building with the raised, vented roof north of the Feast Hall/Museum Building is the Community Kitchen. Women of the Harmony Society used this kitchen to prepare food for the Love Feasts. The interior held large kettles sunk into ovens. The vents in the ceiling allowed the steam to escape. The principal part of a Love Feast was a stew of beef, pork, or lamb, along with rice or *Spaetzle* (German noodles). Roasted ox was also served at special feasts.

The small building north of the Community Kitchen was John Duss's garage. It has been restored as a demonstration blacksmith shop.

4 **THE CABINET SHOP**

The Harmonists had many separate shops for their handicrafts. The Cabinet Shop, also known by the Harmonists at various times as the carpenters shop and the joiners shop, supplied all the doors, windows, and interior trim used to build Economy. It would have been a busy place, as the carpenters made and repaired furniture for over ninety households. Numerous examples of its products are exhibited at Old Economy today. There are lathes on display that were used in the turner's shop, which was possibly housed in an attached addition to the west of the

present building. The Cabinet Shop was used prior to World War I as the wood shop class for Ambridge High School.

The south room of the Cabinet Shop was at one time a clock shop. The Harmonists made a town clock for each of their three communities. The face of the one for Economy is displayed on the Church tower (see pages 16 and 27). The Harmonists also made a clock for the Episcopal church in Pittsburgh and the Wheeling town clock.

Several examples of their work can be seen throughout the site. Much of the detail about these craft shops has been lost, as every year their accounts were taken before the whole Society and, once approved, were burned.

5 THE GRANARY

The Harmonists built three granaries at Economy. The one on the historic site is an oversize version of a Württemberg barn. This building, which they called the *Fructhaus*, was used to store a year's supply of grain to get the Harmonists through the first year of the Millennium, which they believed was imminent. The five-story building is a combination of traditional half-timber and frame construction, with siding above the first floor. It is oriented north-south so the sun would strike the south end more than the longer sides, thus keeping them cooler.

The first floor was used for storage of goods. The other four stories held grain piled on the floor. Later, the first floor was a workroom where Harmonist wine was bottled and a chimney to vent a heating stove was added. Originally, the louvered windows allowed air to circulate to keep the dust of the grain from catching fire by spontaneous combustion.

Another granary was built next to the flour mill, in the northwest corner of town. This granary supplied the flour mill with grain, which was made into flour for sale and use by the Harmonists.

6 BAKE OVEN

Between the Warehouse and the Granary is a Bake Oven. The Harmonists had one on every square. No Harmonist bake ovens survive; this one is based on an oven built by local (Beaver County) German masons during the 1830s and has been placed here for educational purposes. It can hold about forty loaves of bread.

7 WAREHOUSE

West of the Bake Oven is a small building that was first used as the public store before the brick Store was built on the front of the lot, facing Main Street. Diary descriptions suggest that this became the Society's Warehouse, where provisions were distributed to members.

8 PUMP

West of the Warehouse is a water pump—a reproduction of pumps built by the Harmony Society for houses that were not near piped water. The Pump is not at its original location. It has been placed here for educational programs.

9 THE BAKER HOUSE

Located at the far west boundary of the site, this house was originally built for Johannes Langenbacher (J. L. Baker, 1782–1825), the son of the Society's first storekeeper, but he died about the time the house was finished. It became the home of his brother, Gottlieb Romelius Langenbacher (R. L. Baker), who lived there until after George Rapp's death in 1847. He moved to the George Rapp House by 1860.

The Baker House is a typical Harmonist family dwelling at Economy. With a central chimney, it is similar to German houses the Harmonists saw in rural eastern Pennsylvania, particularly in Lancaster County. The first floor has a small, square room used as an entranceway, with a single window and a trapdoor to the root cellar below. Pegboards serve as coat and hat racks. Beside the entranceway and similar in

shape is the kitchen. The stone sink empties through the wall into a slop barrel outside. Originally, the kitchen had a wooden lintel supporting a fireplace in the west wall. This has been removed and a period ten-plate stove installed in its place.

The large main room was a combined living and dining room. The arrangement of furniture is based on a drawing by John Duss. Originally at Economy, the female housekeeper slept in the main room and supervised all of the household and gardening chores for the family. Other women slept upstairs, as did the men. John Duss remembered that when the wooden shed was added onto the back of the house after 1858, all the women lived downstairs.

There would have been about five people in a household. If the number in a house fell below three, households were combined. If a couple had been married before celibacy was adopted, they continued to live in the same house, but as brother and sister. The rest of the household would often be family members. One of the women in the house would be the housekeeper, and the rest of the women would have jobs in the community, mainly in one of the two textile mills. The men had jobs as farmers or in the mills, as craftsmen or tradesmen. Everyone contributed to the household chores and assisted with the Society's planting in the spring and harvesting in the fall. Children attended school until age fourteen, when the boys were apprenticed to learn a craft or trade and the girls were taught

"women's work," or household management.

Perishables were drawn from several places. People got their flour from the flour mill. Most households had their own cow, which supplied milk for the family's daily needs. Surplus milk was collected and taken to the central dairy, where it was processed into butter and cheese. By 1830, a small, hand-drawn cart came around every day to each household and delivered butter and meat. Bread was originally baked by the housekeepers in the indi-

vidual bake ovens but was later supplied from a central bakery. Each household kept its own chickens and used their eggs. Chickens were allowed to run loose, causing occasional quarrels among members. Light laundry for the family was done by the housekeeper. Heavy laundry, such as blankets and sheets, was done in a steam laundry east on Main Street past the hotel. As the members got older, more and more of their necessities were purchased from outside sources.

10 BAKER HOUSE GARDEN

The main entrance of the Baker House opens on the side of the house into the garden. This house and the Lenz House were originally about sixty feet to the west, in the middle of what is now Ohio River Boulevard, and were moved to their present locations in 1960. This reduced the size of the gardens considerably. Every household had its own garden and grew most of its own vegetables. The garden and yard provided a degree of privacy in a community whose members had surrendered a great deal of their individualism.

11 FAMILY SHED

Behind each house was an outbuilding called the Family Shed. Sometimes two houses shared parts of these buildings. Under one roof, the family shed originally held a stable for the cow and the chickens, an outhouse, garden tools, and firewood or, later, coal. Underneath was a second root cellar and above was a barn loft for storing winter hay and drying produce. None of the Harmonist family sheds survive; this one is a reconstruction based on examination of sheds before they were torn down, photographs, and archaeological evidence.

⑫ THE LENZ HOUSE

North of the Baker House is the house of Jonathan Lenz (1807–90), a carpenter. He was one of the intellectuals of the Society and supervised the development of the Economy Oil Company. He was on the board of elders and served as a Junior Trustee (1868–90). Lenz was one of the last of the original Harmonists to die. The Lenz House has been adapted for office use and space for catered meals. It is generally not open to the public.

⑬ THE STORE AND POST OFFICE

The Society generated income by selling its products to the outside world. The Store is where the outside world met the Harmony Society. Almost all sales of Harmonist products, purchases of retail items, and distribution of manufactured goods to members were handled through this building. The counter and shelving arrangement of the Store is based on the memory of Mary Fruth, a nonmember who worked in the Store as a clerk in the 1880s. Storekeeper R. L. Baker was one of the few people in the community who could read and write English, preparing him for his later role as trustee.

If an outside neighbor or farmer had something to sell to the Society, he brought it to the Store. For example, of the twenty or thirty tons of wool the Society bought every year, most was bought outside the community by agents. But many local farmers brought their wool to the storekeeper, who would grade it, record the value in a ledger, and then send the farmer over to the wool warehouse to deliver it. The farmer could purchase necessities at the Store, which would be charged against his account. Such things as felt, leather, shoes, hats, books, glass, tobacco, and cloth were all sold at retail in the Store.

Originally, there was a single space to the west called "werehouse," where bulk goods were kept. Mary Fruth remembered rows of casks and leather harnesses hanging on the wall. Today, the room is divided into three smaller spaces. The room to the south is arranged as a schoolroom (opposite page top right) for Old Economy's student tours.

The room to the north is set up as a doctor's office (bottom right). Initially, the Society had two doctors, Johannes Christoph Müller and William Smith (1789–18?). Both doctors' offices were evidently in their own houses. Müller's office still stands on 14th Street, just three doors down from the Feast Hall/Museum Building. Both doctors left in 1832, during the schism. Conrad Feucht (1800–47), who had been a clerk and later captain of the Society steamboat *Pittsburgh and Wheeling Packet*, then became the doctor. It is not known what training he had, but he served for fifteen years. Feucht left the Society to elope with Hildegart Mutschler (1806–45). They were later permitted to return. After Feucht's death, the Society hired a German-speaking doctor, who came down from Pittsburgh periodically and set up this room as a clinic. The small room next to it may have been a pharmacy. That doctor continued to care for the Harmonists until late in the 1890s.

Behind the Store was the counting room, which is today set up as a post office (opposite page top). The Store originally housed the post office, and eventually the storekeeper became the postmaster. This meant that the Society could handle and control its own mail, as security had been a problem in the past. Mail and newspapers for the neighbors were also handled here. In the early period, there was no delivery, and people went to the post office for their mail. The postmaster had franking privileges, which meant that he could send mail under his own signature without paying postage. This saved the Society a lot of money. The post office desk used by the Society is on display; its cancellation stamp is in the collection.

14 THE MECHANICS BUILDING AND WINE CELLAR

Shops for the shoemaker and tailor were in the center of each of the three towns. This one was called the Mechanics Building. At various times, it held a shoe shop, a tailor shop, and some hatmaking operations. The second story was apparently used as a warehouse. The tailor mainly made clothing for the Society, and little was sold to outsiders. He sat cross-legged sewing his clothes at the large wooden tables inside the shop. The Harmonists had irons cast for them, and several of these and the patterns are on display.

Shoes were made in the shoe shop for Society members, but were also sold to the people in the area. At one time, there were fifteen men working in the shoe shop. All the lasts and equipment here today were used by the Society. The shoe shop continued to operate until about 1908.

Most of the hatmaking took place at the Hat Shop, which was across the street from the Cabinet Shop, but some hat finishing operations were done in the Mechanics Building, preparing them for wholesale. The Harmonists made huge numbers of wool felt hats for men, which they sold mainly in the Store. The Harmonists also made straw hats for the use of the members. They made hats into the 1860s, some of which are in the collection. The hat shop was torn down when the new street system was built in Ambridge after 1902.

The Mechanics Building also contained the printing shop. The press is the oldest printing press in America in its historic location.

Below the Mechanics Building is the high-vaulted Wine

Cellar. This was the main wine cellar of the three at Economy. Some members of the Harmony Society were competent masons and had the skill to make such a vault. As wine was an important staple in the Württemberg diet, the Society originally thought it would be successful producing German wine in America. Though alcoholic beverages were never profitable for the Harmonists, they retailed their surplus beer, hard cider, wine, and whiskey. John Duss sold the right to use the Harmony name to a distillery after he became trustee, and that company lasted until Prohibition in 1920. The Society also made a cure-all medicine out of boneset bitters. John Duss actively promoted this medicine, but it never caught on.

Wine was distributed to members. Each housekeeper went to the Wine Cellar and drew a sufficient amount of wine for her household. After 1870, wine was distributed to paid workers from the wine cellar under the Feast Hall.

This Wine Cellar is about twenty feet deep. The large casks are double tuns and some hold about twelve hundred gallons. The newer casks are reproductions. The Society had a village cooper, who was skilled in making these large casks. Some wine remained in the cellar after the Society was dissolved. During Prohibition, federal and state officials seized at least some of the wine and moved it to a warehouse in Ambridge. Most of the wine was stolen and never seen again. The rest was disposed of about 1940. Two cases of Harmonist wine survive in the collection.

15 GEORGE RAPP GARDEN

In America, George Rapp always had an ornate botanical pleasure garden reminiscent of the gardens of the nobility back in Württemberg. This garden was laid out in a large square, with straight intersecting paths quartering the area. Angular paths divided the quarters.

There are four striking features in the garden. The main feature is a large stone garden house or pavilion, in the center, made up of arches modeled after those of the Renaissance neoclassical architect Andrea Palladio. (A similar arch is on the east door of the Feast Hall/Museum Building.) Originally surmounting the arches were carved wooden baskets of painted fruit by the Pittsburgh artist Joseph Woodwell. Two of the

originals are in the collection. The Pavilion was initially topped with a copper dome. The original building deteriorated and was replaced with the present reproduction. The pond is the original made from Harmony Society bricks. By 1827, the pond contained goldfish that had been purchased in Philadelphia.

Standing in the center of the Pavilion is a wooden statue of *Harmony*. The original was carved by William Rush, considered to be the first American-born sculptor and a relative of the famous Philadelphia physician, Benjamin Rush. Rush started carving ships' figureheads, and his sculptures always had some of that flavor in them. His specialty was figures carved from wood for

fountains, of which this was one. The Society commissioned this sculpture in 1824. It originally stood on a pile of rocks, thirteen feet high. The original statue was holding a lyre, with water springing from the fingers of her upraised hand. The water came from the village water system, which was made up of twenty-five hundred feet of pipes leading from a spring on the hill east of town. The original statue was removed and later placed in the Grotto where it rotted. John Duss allegedly had it burned after he became trustee. The reproduction, made in 1966, is displayed on the statue's original site in the Pavilion.

The second major feature in the garden is the stone Grotto. The Harmonists also built similar structures within mazes in their two other communities, but they were made of brick or wood. The exterior is river stone, but the interior is a domed, coffered ceiling with neoclassical decorations. Frederick Rapp contrasted the rough and natural exterior with the finished and elegant interior. George Rapp came here to meditate. There was a second grotto in the village in the center of a maze, several blocks away.

The third major feature is the mound in the northwest corner, on which grapevines were planted. The Garden once extended west about sixty feet, where Ohio River Boulevard is today. The mound was built from dirt excavated

from the main Wine Cellar beneath the Mechanics Building. Originally, there was a small "pastry house" on top of the hill. The band played from the top of this house for evening gatherings. Later there was a small, sheltered arbor here, where Father Rapp could come to meditate on hot days.

The fourth feature is the garden wall. This is a feature typical of European gardens. It served two purposes. The major purpose was to shelter delicate plants from northern winds. The south side of the wall is warmed by the winter sun; such things as figs could grow in this sheltered place even in western Pennsylvania's harsh climate. Originally the wall had trellises on top to train the branches of fruit trees. The original plantings were fruit trees in disciplined rows, as well as tulips, dahlias, and other flowers, making a memorable spring garden.

Later the Harmonists planted flowering plants along the paths. Their archives show that the Society bought and sold quantities of flowering and ornamental plants. They also propagated orange and lemon trees and dahlia roots.

The first greenhouse was a bark house, protected by what is now called the Vault Wing, the extension on the west side of the George Rapp House. This may have been more of a stove house or orangery. The Harmonists built a second greenhouse close to where the modern one now stands, although the original was considerably larger. John Duss later added to it with an elaborate iron conservatory. The Harmonists were competent botanists, buying or acquiring plants far and wide to grow in the garden as specimens. The George Rapp House had its own kitchen garden about where the present one is. The sundial in the center is a reproduction of one made for this site; the original is in the collection.

Next to the modern greenhouse once stood the village bakery. Originally the Society had a bake oven on each square, but they built a central bakery in the early 1830s. It was used to make bread until the turn of the twentieth century, when it was torn down.

16 THE GEORGE RAPP HOUSE

The George Rapp House, built in 1826, was both the home and office of the leader of the Society. The house was the largest dwelling in Economy, and it reflected the success of the Society and its leader. Its hipped roof is reminiscent of houses in Württemberg. Along Church Street, the continuous facade consists of a two-story central block, flanked by north and south wings. A second house for Frederick Rapp was added to the north. The two houses were joined on the garden side by a continuous porch, two stories high at the center. Under the kitchen was another wine cellar, where Rapp kept special wine he brought from New Harmony. He had been trained as a vinedresser in his youth and continued to have a lifelong interest in viniculture. At various times, friends of Rapp, who acted as stewards for the community, lived in the north wing. Originally, there was no interior passage between the north wing and central block, so the stewards had to go outside and come back in when they took their meals.

The clipped-off ends of the gables, called a sheep's nose, were a common design feature of German buildings. Like the Feast Hall/Museum Building, the foundation of the George Rapp House had a water table with a molded cap course, which helped to direct water away from the masonry joint. Grapevines were trained on trellises in the usual German manner on all but the north wall. Otherwise the building has features common to American brick houses of the late Georgian period.

The central block has a central hall through which one entered the house, balanced with two rooms on each side.

The stairs are entered from the rear of the hall, instead of the front. Originally the stairs were in a separate alcove to the south, off the family reception room. When the stairs were moved, the stair hall space was made part of the sitting room.

The front room south of the hall was the parlor (opposite top). John Duss later called it the Trustees Room, as the trustees had met there every Sunday to plan the week's work, but George Rapp had used it as a drawing room. Displayed are original Harmonist furnishings from the early and mid-nineteenth century. Jacob Henrici and Gertrude Rapp both played the piano, frequently as a duo. The two pianos located in the room had originally been in the church building but were moved here in the 1880s, when the Society bought its first church organ. The large

painting, *Christ Healing the Sick in the Temple*, after the Benjamin West original, was reported by visitors to be hanging in this room by 1829. The chairs and prints were part of the original furnishings of the room. Many travelers, who were guests of the Soci-

ety, commented on the furnishings and the "Philadelphia" wallpaper, fashionable when it was installed in 1826. The room on the garden side was a second parlor. As it was seldom mentioned by travelers, it must have been the private parlor of the Rapp family.

On the north side of the hallway are George Rapp's office and bedroom of his later years (bottom left). He died in the bed that is displayed in the bedroom and delivered his last sermon from the window facing the garden courtyard. The front room is presently exhibited as Jacob Henrici's office (previous page bottom right), where most of the Society's business was conducted after Father Rapp's death. The vault that held the "church fund" of half a million dollars is under this room. The closet and door hid the stone steps that gave access to the vault and cellar under the north wing. The passage through the north stone wall of the central block and the bridge across the stairs were added later in the nineteenth century.

Christina Rapp (1756–1830), George's wife, lived upstairs with their daughter, Rosina Rapp (1786–1849); her granddaughter, Gertraut, or Gertrude (1808–89); and George's sister, Barbara Rapp (1765–1844). By 1849, Gertrude was the only woman living in the house and became its hostess for visiting dignitaries. In the Society, there were no servants that we know of, but the Rapp women took care of the house and were responsible for "women's work," as in the rest of the households.

The south wing contains the dining room, the kitchen (top), and the pantry. The large unusual wine cupboard is original to the dining room. Displayed in the room is the Harmonists' collection of Pittsburgh glass. Gertrude Rapp's bedroom (bottom) was sectioned off from the dining room, apparently when she became too old to climb

the stairs. The kitchen originally had no access to the dining room except through the pantry.

To the south side of the house were a number of support buildings, including a wash house, stable, and shed. George had a small gardener's house in the garden, which was moved a couple blocks away and is now a garage. The small barn where Rapp kept his carriage and horses (above) has been recreated, although the timbers for the upper portion are original. Also on the south side is a well.

The Harmonists were the first to tap into the aquifer that runs under the Ohio River. The original well was over eighty feet deep and was built to supply water before the town system was put in. This pump is a reproduction of the original and is on the exact site.

 THE FREDERICK RAPP HOUSE

In all three villages, Frederick Rapp's house was in the center of the community, with easy access to the public business areas of the village. At Economy, his first house faced Main Street (now 14th Street). This house faces Church Street and is quite imposing, as befits Frederick's status as the business agent of the Society.

Frederick Rapp evidently walked outdoors along the continuous porch to gain access to the George Rapp House for meals and discussions with his father. Frederick had an office in his house where he conducted Society business. He evidently lived alone downstairs in the house. It is reported that he had a private collection of art upstairs in a suite of three large rooms. The only accounts of people meeting Frederick on a social basis were encounters in the George Rapp House. Following Frederick Rapp's death in 1834, the house was used as a dormitory for members of the Society with special duties.

For more information on hours, tours, programs, and activities at
Old Economy Village, visit **www.oldeconomyvillage.org** or call **724-266-4500**.

Further Reading

Arndt, Karl J. R. *George Rapp's Harmony Society, 1785–1847*. Philadelphia: University of Pennsylvania Press, 1965.

———. *George Rapp's Successors and Material Heirs*. Rutherford, N.J., Fairleigh Dickinson University Press, 1971.

Bestor, Arthur. *Backwoods Utopias: The Sectarian Origins and the Owenite Phase of Communitarian Socialism in America, 1663–1829*. 2d rev. ed. Philadelphia: University of Pennsylvania Press, 1970.

Duss, John S. *The Harmonists: A Personal History*. Harrisburg, Pa.: Pennsylvania Book Service, 1943.

Hinds, William A. *American Communities*. 3d ed. Magnolia, Mass.: Peter Smith Publisher, 1991.

Knoedler, Christina F. *The Harmony Society*. New York: Vantage Press, 1954.

Kring, Hilda Adam. *The Harmonists: A Folk-Culture Approach*. Lanham, Md.: Scarecrow Press, 1973.

Mumford, Lewis. *The Story of Utopias*. New York: Corinth Books, 1922.

Nordhoff, Charles. *The Communistic Societies of the United States*. New York: Hillary House, 1875.

Noyes, John Humphrey. *History of American Socialisms*. New York: Hillary House, 1870.

Williams, Aaron. *The Harmony Society at Economy, Pennsylvania*. 1866; reprint, New York: AMS Press, 1960.

Also Available

Anthracite Heritage Museum and Scranton Iron Furnaces

Brandywine Battlefield Park

Conrad Weiser Homestead

Daniel Boone Homestead

Drake Well Museum and Park

Ephrata Cloister

Erie Maritime Museum and U.S. Brig Niagara

Hope Lodge and Mather Mill

Landis Valley Museum

Pennsbury Manor

Railroad Museum of Pennsylvania

All titles are $10, plus shipping, from Stackpole Books, 800-732-3669, www.stackpolebooks.com, or The Pennsylvania Historical and Museum Commission, 800-747-7790, www.phmc.state.pa.us